Apple

Cookbook

Introduction

Welcome to a culinary journey through the delightful world of apples! Apples are one of the most beloved fruits in the world, known for their crisp texture, sweet flavor, and incredible versatility in the kitchen. Whether you're baking a classic apple pie, making a savory pork dish with apple chutney, or simply enjoying a fresh, juicy apple as a snack, there are countless ways to incorporate this delicious fruit into your cooking and baking.

In this cookbook, we'll explore the different varieties of apples, their unique flavor profiles, and how to select the perfect apple for any recipe. We'll also dive into a wide range of sweet and savory dishes that highlight the best of what apples have to offer, from breakfast treats like apple pancakes and muffins, to hearty main courses like apple-stuffed pork chops and roasted chicken with apples and onions.

This cookbook is the ultimate guide to cooking and baking with apples. So whether you're a seasoned chef or a beginner in the kitchen, let's grab some apples and get started on a delicious culinary adventure! 5 minutes before transferring them to a wire rack to cool completely.

Apple Cinnamon Muffins

Ingredients:

2 cups all-purpose flour
1 tbsp. baking powder
1/2 tsp. salt
1 tsp. cinnamon
1/2 cup unsalted butter, softened
1/2 cup granulated sugar
2 large eggs
1/2 cup milk
1 tsp. vanilla extract
2 medium apples, peeled and diced

Directions:

1. Preheat the oven to 375°F (190°C). Grease a muffin tin or line with paper liners.
2. In a medium bowl, whisk together the flour, baking powder, salt, and cinnamon.
3. In a large bowl, beat the butter and sugar together until light and fluffy. Beat in the eggs, one at a time, then stir in the milk and vanilla extract.
4. Add the dry ingredients to the wet ingredients, and stir until just combined. Gently fold in the diced apples.
5. Divide the batter evenly among the muffin cups, filling each about 3/4 full.
6. Bake for 20-25 minutes, or until a toothpick inserted into the center of a muffin comes out clean.
7. Remove the muffins from the oven and allow them to cool in the pan for 5 minutes. Then, transfer them to a wire rack to cool completely.

Apple Bran Muffins

Ingredients:

1 cup all-purpose flour
1 cup wheat bran
1 tsp. baking powder
1/2 tsp. baking soda
1/2 tsp. salt
1/2 tsp. cinnamon
1/4 cup unsalted butter, softened
1/2 cup brown sugar
1 large egg
1 cup unsweetened applesauce
1/4 cup milk
1 tsp. vanilla extract
1 medium apple, peeled and grated
1/4 cup raisins

Directions:

1. Preheat the oven to 375°F (190°C). Grease a muffin tin or line with paper liners.
2. In a medium bowl, whisk together the flour, wheat bran, baking powder, baking soda, salt, and cinnamon.
3. In a large bowl, beat the butter and brown sugar together until light and fluffy. Beat in the egg, then stir in the applesauce, milk, and vanilla extract.
4. Add the dry ingredients to the wet ingredients, and stir until just combined. Gently fold in the grated apple and raisins.
5. Divide the batter evenly among the muffin cups, filling each about 3/4 full.
6. Bake for 20-25 minutes, or until a toothpick inserted into the center of a muffin comes out clean.
7. Remove the muffins from the oven and allow them to cool in the pan for 5 minutes. Then, transfer them to a wire rack to cool completely.

Pumpkin Apple Streusel Muffins

Streusel Topping Ingredients:

1/2 cup all-purpose flour
1/2 cup brown sugar
1/4 cup unsalted butter, melted
1 tsp. cinnamon
1/4 tsp. salt

Muffin Ingredients:

2 cups all-purpose flour
2 tsps. baking powder
1 tsp. baking soda
1 tsp. cinnamon
1/2 tsp. nutmeg
1/2 tsp. salt
1 cup pumpkin puree
1/2 cup brown sugar
1/2 cup vegetable oil
2 large eggs
1 medium apple, peeled and grated
1/4 cup milk

Directions:

1. Preheat the oven to 375°F (190°C). Grease a muffin tin or line with paper liners.
2. Make the streusel topping: In a medium bowl, whisk together the flour, brown sugar, cinnamon, and salt. Stir in the melted butter until the mixture is crumbly.
3. In a large bowl, whisk together the flour, baking powder, baking soda, cinnamon, nutmeg, and salt.
4. In another large bowl, whisk together the pumpkin puree, brown sugar, vegetable oil, eggs, grated apple, and milk.
5. Add the dry ingredients to the wet ingredients, and stir until just combined.

6. Divide the batter evenly among the muffin cups, filling each about 3/4 full.
7. Sprinkle the streusel topping over the top of each muffin, pressing it down gently.
8. Bake for 20-25 minutes, or until a toothpick inserted into the center of a muffin comes out clean.
9. Remove the muffins from the oven and allow them to cool in the pan for 5 minutes. Then, transfer them to a wire rack to cool completely.

Apple Pie Muffins

Muffin Ingredients:

2 cups all-purpose flour
1 tsp. baking powder
1/2 tsp. baking soda
1/2 tsp. salt
1/2 cup unsalted butter, softened
1 cup granulated sugar
2 large eggs
1 tsp. vanilla extract
1/2 cup milk
2 cups chopped apples (peeled and cored)
1 tsp. cinnamon
1/4 tsp. nutmeg

Streusel Topping Ingredients:

1/4 cup all-purpose flour
1/4 cup granulated sugar
1/4 cup unsalted butter, melted
1/2 tsp. cinnamon

Directions:

1. Preheat the oven to 375°F (190°C). Grease a muffin tin or line with paper liners.
2. Make the streusel topping: In a medium bowl, whisk together the flour, sugar, and cinnamon. Stir in the melted butter until the mixture is crumbly.
3. In a large bowl, whisk together the flour, baking powder, baking soda, and salt.
4. In another large bowl, beat the butter and sugar together until light and fluffy. Beat in the eggs and vanilla extract.
5. Gradually add the dry ingredients to the wet ingredients, alternating with the milk, and stir until just combined.
6. Fold in the chopped apples, cinnamon, and nutmeg.

7. Divide the batter evenly among the muffin cups, filling each about 3/4 full.
8. Sprinkle the streusel topping over the top of each muffin, pressing it down gently.
9. Bake for 20-25 minutes, or until a toothpick inserted into the center of a muffin comes out clean.
10. Remove the muffins from the oven and allow them to cool in the pan for 5 minutes. Then, transfer them to a wire rack to cool completely.

Carrot, Apple, and Zucchini Muffins

Ingredients:

1 1/2 cups all-purpose flour
1 tsp. baking powder
1/2 tsp. baking soda
1/2 tsp. salt
1 tsp. cinnamon
1/4 tsp. nutmeg
1/2 cup vegetable oil
1/2 cup granulated sugar
1/4 cup brown sugar
2 large eggs
1 tsp. vanilla extract
1 cup shredded carrot
1 cup shredded apple
1 cup shredded zucchini

Directions:

1. Preheat the oven to 375°F (190°C). Grease a muffin tin or line with paper liners.
2. In a large bowl, whisk together the flour, baking powder, baking soda, salt, cinnamon, and nutmeg.
3. In another large bowl, whisk together the vegetable oil, granulated sugar, brown sugar, eggs, and vanilla extract.
4. Gradually add the dry ingredients to the wet ingredients and stir until just combined.
5. Fold in the shredded carrot, apple, and zucchini.
6. Divide the batter evenly among the muffin cups, filling each about 3/4 full.
7. Bake for 20-25 minutes, or until a toothpick inserted into the center of a muffin comes out clean.
8. Remove the muffins from the oven and allow them to cool in the pan for 5 minutes. Then, transfer them to a wire rack to cool completely.

Apple Carrot Muffins

Ingredients:

1 1/2 cups all-purpose flour
1/2 cup rolled oats
1 tsp. baking powder
1/2 tsp. baking soda
1/2 tsp. salt
1 tsp. ground cinnamon
1/2 tsp. ground ginger
1/4 tsp. ground nutmeg
2 large eggs
1/2 cup unsweetened applesauce
1/4 cup vegetable oil
1/2 cup packed light brown sugar
1 tsp. vanilla extract
1 cup grated carrot
1 cup grated apple (about 1 medium apple)

Directions:

1. Preheat the oven to 375°F (190°C) and line a muffin tin with paper liners.
2. In a large mixing bowl, whisk together the flour, oats, baking powder, baking soda, salt, cinnamon, ginger, and nutmeg.
3. In a separate bowl, whisk together the eggs, applesauce, oil, brown sugar, and vanilla extract.
4. Add the wet ingredients to the dry ingredients and stir until just combined.
5. Fold in the grated carrot and apple.
6. Spoon the batter into the prepared muffin tin, filling each cup about 2/3 full.
7. Bake for 18-20 minutes, or until a toothpick inserted into the center of a muffin comes out clean.
8. Allow the muffins to cool in the pan for 5 minutes before transferring them to a wire rack to cool completely.

Apple Cinnamon Baked Oatmeal

Ingredients:

2 cups rolled oats
1/2 cup chopped walnuts
1/2 cup raisins
1 tsp. baking powder
1/2 tsp. salt
1 tsp. cinnamon
2 cups milk
1/2 cup applesauce
1/4 cup maple syrup
1 large egg
2 tbsps. unsalted butter, melted
1 tsp. vanilla extract
1 large apple, peeled and diced

Directions:

1. Preheat the oven to 375°F (190°C). Grease a 9-inch square baking dish.
2. In a large bowl, mix together the rolled oats, chopped walnuts, raisins, baking powder, salt, and cinnamon.
3. In another large bowl, whisk together the milk, applesauce, maple syrup, egg, melted butter, and vanilla extract.
4. Pour the wet ingredients into the bowl with the dry ingredients and stir until well combined.
5. Fold in the diced apple.
6. Pour the mixture into the prepared baking dish.
7. Bake for 35-40 minutes, or until the top is golden brown and the oatmeal is set.
8. Remove from the oven and let it cool for 5-10 minutes before serving.

Cranberry Cream Cheese Stuffed Apples

Ingredients:

4 large apples
4 oz cream cheese, softened
1/4 cup dried cranberries
2 tbsps. honey
1 tsp. cinnamon
1/4 tsp. nutmeg
1/4 cup chopped walnuts

Directions:

1. Preheat the oven to 375°F (190°C). Line a baking sheet with parchment paper.
2. Cut off the top 1/4 of each apple, then use a spoon or melon baller to scoop out the core and seeds, leaving a hollow cavity in each apple.
3. In a medium bowl, stir together the cream cheese, dried cranberries, honey, cinnamon, and nutmeg until well combined.
4. Spoon the cream cheese mixture into the hollowed-out apples, dividing it evenly among them.
5. Sprinkle the chopped walnuts over the top of the cream cheese mixture.
6. Place the stuffed apples on the prepared baking sheet and bake for 20-25 minutes, or until the apples are tender and the filling is hot and bubbly.
7. Serve the stuffed apples warm, garnished with additional chopped walnuts and a drizzle of honey, if desired.

Baked Apples Stuffed with Cinnamon Oatmeal

Ingredients:

4 large apples, cored
1 cup rolled oats
1/2 cup almond milk
1/4 cup maple syrup
1 tsp. cinnamon
1/4 tsp. nutmeg
1/4 tsp. salt
1/4 cup chopped walnuts

Directions:

1. Preheat the oven to 375°F (190°C).
2. In a large bowl, mix together the rolled oats, almond milk, maple syrup, cinnamon, nutmeg, salt, and chopped walnuts.
3. Stuff the cored apples with the oatmeal mixture and place them in a baking dish.
4. Bake for 30-35 minutes, or until the apples are tender and the oatmeal is golden brown.

Stuffed Apples with Quinoa and Feta Cheese

Ingredients:

4 large apples, cored
1 cup cooked quinoa
1/4 cup crumbled feta cheese
1/4 cup chopped fresh parsley
1/4 cup chopped walnuts
1/4 tsp. salt
1/4 tsp. black pepper

Directions:

1. Preheat the oven to 375°F (190°C).
2. In a large bowl, mix together the cooked quinoa, crumbled feta cheese, chopped parsley, chopped walnuts, salt, and black pepper.
3. Stuff the cored apples with the quinoa mixture and place them in a baking dish.
4. Bake for 25-30 minutes, or until the apples are tender and the quinoa is heated through.

Stuffed Apples with Sausage and Gouda Cheese

Ingredients:

4 large apples, cored
1/2 pound ground sausage
1/2 cup shredded gouda cheese
1/4 cup chopped green onions
1/4 tsp. salt
1/4 tsp. black pepper

Directions:

1. Preheat the oven to 375°F (190°C).
2. In a large skillet, cook the ground sausage over medium heat until browned and cooked through.
3. Remove from the heat and stir in the shredded gouda cheese, chopped green onions, salt, and black pepper.
4. Stuff the cored apples with the sausage mixture and place them in a baking dish.
5. Bake for 30-35 minutes, or until the apples are tender and the sausage mixture is golden brown.

Stuffed Apples with Caramelized Onions and Goat Cheese

Ingredients:

4 large apples, cored
2 tbsps. butter
2 large onions, thinly sliced
1/4 tsp. salt
1/4 tsp. black pepper
4 oz. goat cheese, crumbled

Directions:

1. Preheat the oven to 375°F (190°C).
2. In a large skillet, melt the butter over medium heat.
3. Add the sliced onions and cook until caramelized, about 20-25 minutes.
4. Season with salt and black pepper.
5. Stuff the cored apples with the caramelized onions and crumbled goat cheese.
6. Place the stuffed apples in a baking dish and bake for 25-30 minutes, or until the apples are tender and the goat cheese is melted and golden brown.

Stuffed Apples with Almond Butter and Chocolate Chips

Ingredients:

4 large apples, cored
1/2 cup almond butter
1/4 cup chocolate chips
1/4 cup chopped almonds

Directions:

1. Preheat the oven to 375°F (190°C).
2. In a small bowl, mix together the almond butter and chocolate chips.
3. Stuff the cored apples with the almond butter and chocolate chip mixture.
4. Place the stuffed apples in a baking dish and sprinkle with chopped almonds.
5. Bake for 25-30 minutes, or until the apples are tender and the almond butter and chocolate chips are melted and gooey.
6. Serve warm and enjoy!

Classic Apple Pie

Ingredients:

1 double pie crust recipe
8 cups peeled and sliced apples
1/2 cup granulated sugar
1/4 cup brown sugar
1 tbsp. lemon juice
1 tsp. ground cinnamon
1/4 tsp. ground nutmeg
1/4 tsp. salt
2 tbsps. unsalted butter, cut into small pieces
1 egg, beaten

Directions:

1. Preheat the oven to 375°F (190°C).
2. In a large bowl, mix together the sliced apples, granulated sugar, brown sugar, lemon juice, cinnamon, nutmeg, and salt.
3. Roll out one of the pie crusts and place it in a 9-inch pie dish.
4. Add the apple mixture to the pie crust, and dot with small pieces of butter.
5. Roll out the second pie crust and place it on top of the apple mixture. Trim the edges of the crust and crimp to seal.
6. Brush the top of the pie with the beaten egg.
7. Cut several slits in the top of the pie crust to allow steam to escape.
8. Bake for 45-50 minutes, or until the crust is golden brown and the filling is bubbling.
9. Let cool for 10 minutes before slicing and serving.

Dutch Apple Pie

Ingredients:

1 double pie crust recipe
8 cups peeled and sliced apples
1/2 cup granulated sugar
1/4 cup brown sugar
1 tbsp. lemon juice
1 tsp. ground cinnamon
1/4 tsp. ground nutmeg
1/4 tsp. salt
1/2 cup all-purpose flour
1/2 cup unsalted butter, cut into small pieces
1 cup old-fashioned rolled oats
1/2 cup chopped walnuts

Directions:

1. Preheat the oven to 375°F (190°C).
2. In a large bowl, mix together the sliced apples, granulated sugar, brown sugar, lemon juice, cinnamon, nutmeg, and salt.
3. Roll out one of the pie crusts and place it in a 9-inch pie dish.
4. Add the apple mixture to the pie crust.
5. In a separate bowl, mix together the flour, butter, rolled oats, and chopped walnuts until crumbly.
6. Sprinkle the crumb mixture over the top of the apple mixture.
7. Roll out the second pie crust and place it on top of the crumb mixture. Trim the edges of the crust and crimp to seal.
8. Cut several slits in the top of the pie crust to allow steam to escape.
9. Bake for 45-50 minutes, or until the crust is golden brown and the filling is bubbling.
10. Let cool for 10 minutes before slicing and serving.

Caramel Apple Pie

Ingredients:

1 double pie crust recipe
8 cups peeled and sliced apples
1/2 cup granulated sugar
1/4 cup brown sugar
1 tbsp. lemon juice
1 tsp. ground cinnamon
1/4 tsp. ground nutmeg
1/4 tsp. salt
1/4 cup unsalted butter
1/2 cup heavy cream
1/2 cup caramel sauce

Directions:

1. Preheat the oven to 375°F (190°C).
2. In a large bowl, mix together the sliced apples, granulated sugar, brown sugar, lemon juice, cinnamon, nutmeg, and salt.
3. Roll out one of the pie crusts and place it in a 9-inch pie dish.
4. Add the apple mixture to the pie crust, and dot with small pieces of butter.
5. In a small saucepan, heat the heavy cream and caramel sauce over low heat, stirring constantly, until the mixture is smooth and heated through.
6. Pour the caramel mixture over the top of the apples in the pie crust.
7. Roll out the second pie crust and place it on top of the caramel mixture. Trim the edges of the crust and crimp to seal.
8. Cut several slits in the top of the pie crust to allow steam to escape.
9. Bake for 45-50 minutes, or until the crust is golden brown and the filling is bubbling.

10. Let cool for 10 minutes before slicing and serving.

Apple Crumb Pie

Ingredients:

1 double pie crust recipe
8 cups peeled and sliced apples
1/2 cup granulated sugar
1/4 cup brown sugar
1 tbsp. lemon juice
1 tsp. ground cinnamon
1/4 tsp. ground nutmeg
1/4 tsp. salt
1/2 cup all-purpose flour
1/2 cup unsalted butter, melted
1/2 cup old-fashioned rolled oats
1/2 cup chopped pecans

Directions:

1. Preheat the oven to 375°F (190°C).
2. In a large bowl, mix together the sliced apples, granulated sugar, brown sugar, lemon juice, cinnamon, nutmeg, and salt.
3. Roll out one of the pie crusts and place it in a 9-inch pie dish.
4. Add the apple mixture to the pie crust.
5. In a separate bowl, mix together the flour, melted butter, rolled oats, and chopped pecans until crumbly.
6. Sprinkle the crumb mixture over the top of the apple mixture.
7. Roll out the second pie crust and place it on top of the crumb mixture. Trim the edges of the crust and crimp to seal.
8. Cut several slits in the top of the pie crust to allow steam to escape.
9. Bake for 45-50 minutes, or until the crust is golden brown and the filling is bubbling.
10. Let cool for 10 minutes before slicing and serving.

Apple Cranberry Pie

Ingredients:

1 double pie crust recipe
8 cups peeled and sliced apples
1 cup fresh or frozen cranberries
1/2 cup granulated sugar
1/4 cup brown sugar
1 tbsp. lemon juice
1 tsp. ground cinnamon
1/4 tsp. ground nutmeg
1/4 tsp. salt
2 tbsps. unsalted butter, cut into small pieces
1 egg, beaten

Directions:

1. Preheat the oven to 375°F (190°C).
2. In a large bowl, mix together the sliced apples, cranberries, granulated sugar, brown sugar, lemon juice, cinnamon, nutmeg, and salt.
3. Roll out one of the pie crusts and place it in a 9-inch pie dish.
4. Add the apple and cranberry mixture to the pie crust, and dot with small pieces of butter.
5. Roll out the second pie crust and place it on top of the apple and cranberry mixture. Trim the edges of the crust and crimp to seal.
6. Brush the top of the pie with the beaten egg.
7. Cut several slits in the top of the pie crust to allow steam to escape.
8. Bake for 45-50 minutes, or until the crust is golden brown and the filling is bubbling.
9. Let cool for 10 minutes before slicing and serving.

Classic Apple Slaw

Ingredients:

1/2 head green cabbage, thinly sliced
1 large carrot, grated
1 Granny Smith apple, cored and thinly sliced
1/4 cup mayonnaise
1 tbsp. Dijon mustard
1 tbsp. apple cider vinegar
1 tbsp. honey
Salt and pepper, to taste

Directions:

1. In a large bowl, combine the cabbage, carrot, and apple.
2. In a small bowl, whisk together the mayonnaise, mustard, apple cider vinegar, honey, salt, and pepper.
3. Pour the dressing over the cabbage mixture and toss to combine.
4. Chill in the refrigerator for at least 30 minutes before serving.

Waldorf Apple Slaw

Ingredients:

1/2 head green cabbage, thinly sliced
1 large carrot, grated
2 Granny Smith apples, cored and thinly sliced
1/2 cup chopped walnuts
1/2 cup raisins
1/4 cup mayonnaise
1/4 cup plain Greek yogurt
2 tbsps. apple cider vinegar
1 tbsp. honey
Salt and pepper, to taste

Directions:

1. In a large bowl, combine the cabbage, carrot, apple, walnuts, and raisins.
2. In a small bowl, whisk together the mayonnaise, Greek yogurt, apple cider vinegar, honey, salt, and pepper.
3. Pour the dressing over the cabbage mixture and toss to combine.
4. Chill in the refrigerator for at least 30 minutes before serving.

Spicy Apple Slaw

Ingredients:

1/2 head red cabbage, thinly sliced
1 large carrot, grated
2 Granny Smith apples, cored and thinly sliced
1/4 cup chopped fresh cilantro
1 jalapeño pepper, seeded and finely chopped
1/4 cup mayonnaise
1/4 cup sour cream
2 tbsps. lime juice
1 tbsp. honey
Salt and pepper, to taste

Directions:

1. In a large bowl, combine the red cabbage, carrot, apple, cilantro, and jalapeño pepper.
2. In a small bowl, whisk together the mayonnaise, sour cream, lime juice, honey, salt, and pepper.
3. Pour the dressing over the cabbage mixture and toss to combine.
4. Chill in the refrigerator for at least 30 minutes before serving.

Asian Apple Slaw

Ingredients:

1/2 head Napa cabbage, thinly sliced
1 large carrot, grated
2 Granny Smith apples, cored and thinly sliced
1/4 cup chopped fresh cilantro
1/4 cup chopped roasted peanuts
2 tbsps. rice vinegar
2 tbsps. soy sauce
1 tbsp. sesame oil
1 tbsp. honey
1 garlic clove, minced

Directions:

1. In a large bowl, combine the Napa cabbage, carrot, apple, cilantro, and roasted peanuts.
2. In a small bowl, whisk together the rice vinegar, soy sauce, sesame oil, honey, and garlic.
3. Pour the dressing over the cabbage mixture and toss to combine.
4. Chill in the refrigerator for at least 30 minutes before serving.

Apple and Jicama Slaw

Ingredients:

1/2 head red cabbage, thinly sliced
1 large jicama, peeled and thinly sliced
2 Granny Smith apples, cored and thinly sliced
1/4 cup chopped fresh cilantro
2 tbsps. lime juice
1 tbsp. honey
Salt and pepper, to taste

Directions:

1. In a large bowl, combine the red cabbage, jicama, apple, and cilantro.
2. In a small bowl, whisk together the lime juice, honey, salt, and pepper.
3. Pour the dressing over the cabbage mixture and toss to combine.
4. Chill in the refrigerator for at least 30 minutes before serving.

Kohlrabi and Apple Slaw

Ingredients:

1 kohlrabi, peeled and julienned
2 apples, cored and julienned
1/2 red onion, thinly sliced
1/4 cup chopped fresh parsley
1/4 cup chopped fresh mint
1/4 cup apple cider vinegar
2 tbsps. honey
1/4 cup olive oil
Salt and pepper to taste

Directions:

1. In a large mixing bowl, whisk together the apple cider vinegar, honey, olive oil, salt, and pepper to make the dressing.
2. Add the kohlrabi, apples, red onion, parsley, and mint to the bowl. Toss well to coat everything with the dressing.
3. Cover and refrigerate for at least 30 minutes before serving to allow the flavors to meld together.
4. Enjoy!

Purple Apple Slaw

Ingredients:

1 small head of purple cabbage, thinly sliced
2 medium-sized apples, cored and sliced into thin matchsticks
1/2 cup shredded carrots
1/4 cup chopped fresh parsley
1/4 cup chopped fresh mint
1/4 cup apple cider vinegar
2 tbsp honey
2 tbsp Dijon mustard
1/4 cup olive oil
Salt and pepper, to taste

Directions:

1. In a large bowl, combine the sliced purple cabbage, apple matchsticks, shredded carrots, parsley, and mint.
2. In a separate small bowl, whisk together the apple cider vinegar, honey, Dijon mustard, and olive oil until smooth.
3. Pour the dressing over the cabbage mixture and toss to coat evenly.
4. Season with salt and pepper to taste.
5. Let the slaw sit in the refrigerator for at least 30 minutes before serving to allow the flavors to meld together.
6. Serve chilled and enjoy!

Waldorf Salad

Ingredients:

2 apples, cored and diced
1 cup of red seedless grapes, halved
1 cup of diced celery
1 cup of chopped walnuts
1/2 cup of mayonnaise
1/4 cup of sour cream
2 tbsps. of fresh lemon juice
Salt and pepper to taste
Lettuce leaves for serving

Directions:

1. In a large bowl, mix together the diced apples, halved grapes, diced celery, and chopped walnuts.
2. In a separate bowl, whisk together the mayonnaise, sour cream, and lemon juice until smooth. Season with salt and pepper to taste.
3. Pour the dressing over the apple mixture and toss to coat evenly.
4. Chill the salad in the refrigerator for at least 30 minutes.
5. To serve, arrange lettuce leaves on a plate and spoon the chilled salad over the top.

Apple and Fennel Salad

Ingredients:

2 Granny Smith apples, cored and thinly sliced
1 small fennel bulb, thinly sliced
1/4 cup chopped fresh parsley
1/4 cup extra-virgin olive oil
2 tbsps. apple cider vinegar
1 tbsp. honey
Salt and pepper to taste

Directions:

1. In a large bowl, toss together the sliced apples, fennel, and parsley. In a separate bowl, whisk together the olive oil, apple cider vinegar, honey, salt, and pepper until well combined. Drizzle the dressing over the salad and toss to coat evenly. Serve immediately.

Apple and Cheddar Salad

Ingredients:

2 Granny Smith apples, cored and thinly sliced
4 cups mixed greens
1/2 cup chopped walnuts
1/2 cup crumbled cheddar cheese
1/4 cup apple cider vinegar
1/4 cup extra-virgin olive oil
1 tbsp. Dijon mustard
Salt and pepper to taste

Directions:

1. In a large bowl, toss together the sliced apples, mixed greens, walnuts, and cheddar cheese. In a separate bowl, whisk together the apple cider vinegar, olive oil, Dijon mustard, salt, and pepper until well combined. Drizzle the dressing over the salad and toss to coat evenly. Serve immediately.

Apple and Cranberry Salad

Ingredients:

2 Granny Smith apples, cored and diced
1 cup dried cranberries
1/2 cup chopped pecans
4 cups baby spinach
1/4 cup apple cider vinegar
1/4 cup extra-virgin olive oil
2 tbsps. honey
Salt and pepper to taste

Directions:

1. In a large bowl, toss together the diced apples, dried
    cranberries, chopped pecans, and baby spinach. In a
    separate bowl, whisk together the apple cider vinegar,
    olive oil, honey, salt, and pepper until well combined.
    Drizzle the dressing over the salad and toss to coat
    evenly. Serve immediately.

Apple and Quinoa Salad

Ingredients:

2 Granny Smith apples, cored and diced
1 cup cooked quinoa
1/2 cup crumbled feta cheese
1/4 cup chopped fresh mint
1/4 cup extra-virgin olive oil
2 tbsps. lemon juice
1 tbsp. honey
Salt and pepper to taste

Directions:

1. In a large bowl, toss together the diced apples, cooked quinoa, crumbled feta cheese, and fresh mint. In a separate bowl, whisk together the olive oil, lemon juice, honey, salt, and pepper until well combined. Drizzle the dressing over the salad and toss to coat evenly. Serve immediately.

Apple and Chicken Salad

Ingredients:

2 Granny Smith apples, cored and diced
2 cups cooked shredded chicken
1/2 cup chopped celery
1/4 cup chopped fresh parsley
1/4 cup plain Greek yogurt
1/4 cup mayonnaise
1 tbsp. Dijon mustard
Salt and pepper to taste

Directions:

1. In a large bowl, toss together the diced apples, shredded chicken, celery, and parsley. In a separate bowl, whisk together the Greek yogurt, mayonnaise, Dijon mustard, salt, and pepper until well combined. Drizzle the dressing over the salad and toss to coat evenly. Serve immediately.

Pumpkin Apple Salad

Ingredients:

1 small pumpkin, peeled, seeded, and cut into small cubes
2 apples, cored and chopped
1/2 cup walnuts, chopped
1/4 cup crumbled goat cheese
4 cups mixed greens
1/4 cup apple cider vinegar
2 tbsps. honey
1/4 cup olive oil
Salt and pepper to taste

Directions:

1. Preheat oven to 375°F (190°C).
2. Place the pumpkin cubes on a baking sheet and drizzle with olive oil. Season with salt and pepper. Roast for 20-25 minutes, or until tender and slightly caramelized.
3. In a large mixing bowl, whisk together the apple cider vinegar, honey, olive oil, salt, and pepper to make the dressing.
4. Add the mixed greens, apples, walnuts, and roasted pumpkin cubes to the bowl. Toss well to coat everything with the dressing.
5. Sprinkle the crumbled goat cheese on top of the salad and serve.

Apple Dumplings

Ingredients:

2 cups all-purpose flour
1/2 tsp. salt
2/3 cup shortening or butter
5 to 7 tbsps. cold water
6 medium-sized apples
6 tbsps. unsalted butter, cut into small pieces
6 tbsps. brown sugar
1 tsp. ground cinnamon
1/4 tsp. ground nutmeg
1 1/2 cups water
1 cup granulated sugar

Directions:

1. Preheat the oven to 375°F (190°C).
2. In a large mixing bowl, combine the flour and salt. Cut in the shortening or butter until the mixture resembles coarse crumbs.
3. Gradually add the cold water, 1 tbsp. at a time, and stir until the dough forms a ball.
4. On a lightly floured surface, roll out the dough into a large rectangle. Cut the dough into 6 equal pieces.
5. Peel and core the apples, then place an apple in the center of each piece of dough.
6. Combine the brown sugar, cinnamon, and nutmeg, and sprinkle over the apples. Top each apple with a small piece of butter.
7. Fold the dough around each apple, pinching the seams together to seal them.
8. Place the apple dumplings in a baking dish.
9. In a saucepan, combine the water and granulated sugar. Bring to a boil, stirring constantly, until the sugar dissolves.
10. Pour the sugar syrup over the apple dumplings.

11. Bake for 35 to 45 minutes, or until the dumplings are golden brown and the apples are tender.
12. Serve the apple dumplings warm, with a scoop of vanilla ice cream or a drizzle of heavy cream, if desired.

Rice Stuffing with Apples, Herbs, and Bacon

Ingredients:

1 cup long-grain white rice
2 cups chicken broth
6 slices of bacon, chopped
1 onion, diced
2 celery stalks, diced
2 apples, cored and diced
2 garlic cloves, minced
1 tbsp. fresh thyme leaves
1 tbsp. fresh sage leaves, chopped
Salt and pepper to taste

Directions:

1. Preheat the oven to 375°F (190°C).
2. In a medium saucepan, bring the chicken broth to a boil. Add the rice and stir to combine. Reduce the heat to low, cover, and simmer for 18-20 minutes, or until the rice is tender and the liquid is absorbed.
3. In a large skillet over medium heat, cook the chopped bacon until crisp. Using a slotted spoon, transfer the bacon to a paper towel-lined plate and set aside.
4. In the same skillet, add the diced onion, celery, and apples. Cook for 5-7 minutes, or until the vegetables are tender.
5. Add the minced garlic, thyme, sage, salt, and pepper to the skillet. Cook for an additional minute, stirring frequently.
6. Add the cooked rice and the reserved bacon to the skillet, stirring to combine.
7. Transfer the rice stuffing to a large baking dish. Cover the dish with aluminum foil and bake for 25-30 minutes, or until heated through.

8. Remove the aluminum foil and bake for an additional 5-10 minutes, or until the top is lightly browned.
9. Serve the rice stuffing hot as a side dish with your favorite main course.

Apple and Sausage Stuffing

Ingredients:

1 loaf of white bread, cut into small cubes
1 lb. ground sausage
1 onion, chopped
3 celery stalks, chopped
2 apples, cored and chopped
2 garlic cloves, minced
1 tbsp. fresh thyme leaves
1 tbsp. fresh sage leaves, chopped
2 cups chicken broth
2 eggs, beaten
Salt and pepper to taste

Directions:

1. Preheat oven to 375°F (190°C).
2. In a large skillet, cook the sausage until browned. Remove the sausage from the skillet and set aside.
3. In the same skillet, cook the onion, celery, and apples until the vegetables are tender.
4. Add the garlic, thyme, and sage to the skillet. Cook for another minute, stirring frequently.
5. In a large mixing bowl, combine the bread cubes, sausage, vegetable mixture, chicken broth, and beaten eggs. Mix well.
6. Transfer the stuffing mixture to a baking dish. Cover with foil and bake for 30 minutes. Remove the foil and bake for an additional 10-15 minutes, or until the top is golden brown.

Apple and Walnut Stuffing

Ingredients:

1 loaf of sourdough bread, cut into small cubes
1 onion, chopped
2 celery stalks, chopped
2 apples, cored and chopped
1 cup chopped walnuts
1 tbsp. fresh thyme leaves
1 tbsp. fresh rosemary leaves, chopped
2 cups chicken broth
2 eggs, beaten
Salt and pepper to taste

Directions:

1. Preheat oven to 375°F (190°C).
2. In a large skillet, cook the onion, celery, and apples until the vegetables are tender.
3. In a large mixing bowl, combine the bread cubes, vegetable mixture, walnuts, thyme, rosemary, chicken broth, and beaten eggs. Mix well.
4. Transfer the stuffing mixture to a baking dish. Cover with foil and bake for 30 minutes. Remove the foil and bake for an additional 10-15 minutes, or until the top is golden brown.

Apple, Bacon, and Cornbread Stuffing

Ingredients:

1 package of cornbread mix, prepared according to package instructions and cut into small cubes
6 slices of bacon, chopped
1 onion, chopped
2 celery stalks, chopped
2 apples, cored and chopped
1 tbsp. fresh thyme leaves
2 cups chicken broth
Salt and pepper to taste

Directions:

1. Preheat oven to 375°F (190°C).
2. In a large skillet, cook the bacon until crisp. Remove the bacon from the skillet and set aside.
3. In the same skillet, cook the onion, celery, and apples until the vegetables are tender.
4. In a large mixing bowl, combine the cornbread cubes, bacon, vegetable mixture, thyme, chicken broth, salt, and pepper. Mix well.
5. Transfer the stuffing mixture to a baking dish. Cover with foil and bake for 30 minutes. Remove the foil and bake for an additional 10-15 minutes, or until the top is golden brown.

Apple, Cranberry, and Pecan Stuffing

Ingredients:

1 loaf of white bread, cut into small cubes
1 onion, chopped
2 celery stalks, chopped
2 apples, cored and chopped
1 cup dried cranberries
1 cup chopped pecans
1 tbsp. fresh thyme leaves
1 tbsp. fresh sage leaves, chopped
2 cups chicken broth
2 eggs, beaten
Salt and pepper to taste

1. Directions:

2. Preheat oven to 375°F (190°C).
3. In a large skillet, cook the onion, celery, and apples until the vegetables are tender.
4. In a large mixing bowl, combine the bread cubes, vegetable mixture, cranberries, pecans, thyme, sage, chicken broth, and beaten eggs. Mix well.
5. Transfer the stuffing mixture to a baking dish. Cover with foil and bake for 30 minutes. Remove the foil and bake for an additional 10-15 minutes, or until the top is golden brown.

Apple and Corn Stuffing

Ingredients:

1 loaf of white bread, cut into small cubes
1 onion, chopped
2 celery stalks, chopped
2 apples, cored and chopped
1 cup corn kernels
1 tbsp. fresh thyme leaves
2 cups chicken broth
2 eggs, beaten
Salt and pepper to taste

Directions:

1. Preheat oven to 375°F (190°C).
2. In a large skillet, cook the onion, celery, and apples until the vegetables are tender.
3. In a large mixing bowl, combine the bread cubes, vegetable mixture, corn kernels, thyme, chicken broth, and beaten eggs. Mix well.
4. Transfer the stuffing mixture to a baking dish. Cover with foil and bake for 30 minutes. Remove the foil and bake for an additional 10-15 minutes, or until the top is golden brown.

Sausage, Apple and Cranberry Stuffing

Ingredients:

1 lb. ground sausage
1 onion, chopped
2 celery stalks, chopped
2 apples, cored and chopped
1 cup dried cranberries
1 tbsp. fresh sage leaves, chopped
1 tbsp. fresh thyme leaves
1 loaf of white bread, cut into small cubes
2 cups chicken broth
2 eggs, beaten
Salt and pepper to taste

Directions:

1. Preheat oven to 375°F (190°C).
2. In a large skillet, cook the sausage until browned, breaking it up into small pieces with a spatula as it cooks.
3. Add the onion and celery to the skillet and cook until the vegetables are tender.
4. In a large mixing bowl, combine the bread cubes, sausage mixture, apples, cranberries, sage, thyme, chicken broth, and beaten eggs. Mix well.
5. Transfer the stuffing mixture to a baking dish. Cover with foil and bake for 30 minutes. Remove the foil and bake for an additional 10-15 minutes, or until the top is golden brown.

Classic Applesauce

Ingredients:

6 medium-sized apples, peeled, cored, and chopped
1/2 cup water
1/4 cup sugar
1/2 tsp. cinnamon
Pinch of salt

Directions:

1. Combine all ingredients in a large pot.
2. Bring to a boil, then reduce heat and simmer for 20-25 minutes, or until the apples are very tender.
3. Use a potato masher or immersion blender to mash the apples to your desired consistency.
4. Serve warm or chilled.

Cinnamon Applesauce

Ingredients:

6 medium-sized apples
1/2 cup water
1/4 cup granulated sugar
1 tsp ground cinnamon
1/4 tsp ground nutmeg
1 pinch of salt

Directions:

1. Peel, core, and chop the apples into small pieces.
2. In a large saucepan, combine the chopped apples, water, sugar, cinnamon, nutmeg, and salt.
3. Cook over medium heat, stirring occasionally, until the apples are soft and tender. This should take about 15-20 minutes.
4. Remove from heat and let the mixture cool for a few minutes.
5. Using an immersion blender, puree the apple mixture until it reaches a smooth and creamy consistency.
6. Serve warm or cold, as desired.

Ginger Applesauce

Ingredients:

6 medium-sized apples
1/2 cup water
1/4 cup granulated sugar
2 tbsp fresh ginger, grated
1 tsp ground cinnamon
Pinch of salt

Directions:

1. Peel, core, and chop the apples into small pieces.
2. In a large saucepan, combine the chopped apples, water, sugar, ginger, cinnamon, and salt.
3. Cook over medium heat, stirring occasionally, until the apples are soft and tender. This should take about 15-20 minutes.
4. Remove from heat and let the mixture cool for a few minutes.
5. Using an immersion blender, puree the apple mixture until it reaches a smooth and creamy consistency.
6. Serve warm or cold, as desired.
7. You can store the ginger apple sauce in an airtight container in the refrigerator for up to a week. The sauce can be used as a topping for pancakes or waffles, as a filling for pies or tarts, or as a snack on its own. Enjoy!

Maple Applesauce

Ingredients:

6 medium-sized apples
1/2 cup water
1/4 cup pure maple syrup
1 tsp ground cinnamon
Pinch of salt

Directions:

1. Peel, core, and chop the apples into small pieces.
2. In a large saucepan, combine the chopped apples, water, maple syrup, cinnamon, and salt.
3. Cook over medium heat, stirring occasionally, until the apples are soft and tender. This should take about 15-20 minutes.
4. Remove from heat and let the mixture cool for a few minutes.
5. Using an immersion blender, puree the apple mixture until it reaches a smooth and creamy consistency.
6. Serve warm or cold, as desired.

Spiced Applesauce

Ingredients:

6 medium-sized apples
1/2 cup water
1/4 cup granulated sugar
1 tsp ground cinnamon
1/4 tsp ground nutmeg
1/4 tsp ground cloves
Pinch of salt

Directions:

1. Peel, core, and chop the apples into small pieces.
2. In a large saucepan, combine the chopped apples, water, sugar, cinnamon, nutmeg, cloves, and salt.
3. Cook over medium heat, stirring occasionally, until the apples are soft and tender. This should take about 15-20 minutes.
4. Remove from heat and let the mixture cool for a few minutes.
5. Using an immersion blender, puree the apple mixture until it reaches a smooth and creamy consistency.
6. Serve warm or cold, as desired.
7. You can store the spiced apple sauce in an airtight container in the refrigerator for up to a week. The sauce can be used as a topping for ice cream or pancakes, as a filling for pies or turnovers, or as a side dish. Enjoy!

Red Hot Applesauce

Ingredients:

6 apples - peeled, cored, and chopped
1/4 cup water
1/4 cup cinnamon candies (such as Red Hots)
2 tbsps. white sugar

Directions:

1. Combine apples and water in a large pot over medium heat.
2. Bring to a simmer and cook for 5 minutes.
3. Stir cinnamon candies and sugar into the apples and water; return mixture to a simmer and cook until the candies melt, about 15 minutes.
4. Remove pot from heat and set aside until the mixture cools, about 15 minutes.
5. Mash apples with a potato masher until no large chunks remain.
6. Alternately, you can blend the mixture with an immersion blender to get a smoother applesauce.

Cinnamon Orange Applesauce

Ingredients:

6 medium apples, peeled, cored, and sliced
1/4 cup water
1/4 cup orange juice
1 tbsp. honey
1/2 tsp. ground cinnamon
1/4 tsp. ground nutmeg
1 pinch of salt

Directions:

1. In a large saucepan, combine the sliced apples, water, and orange juice. Bring to a boil over medium-high heat.
2. Reduce the heat to low, cover the pan, and simmer for 10-15 minutes, or until the apples are tender.
3. Remove the pan from the heat and let it cool for a few minutes.
4. Using an immersion blender or a food processor, puree the apples until smooth.
5. Return the pan to the stove and add the honey, cinnamon, nutmeg, and salt. Stir to combine.
6. Cook over low heat for 5-10 minutes, stirring occasionally, until the applesauce is thickened and heated through.
7. Remove the pan from the heat and let the applesauce cool to room temperature.
8. Serve the cinnamon orange applesauce as a snack or a dessert, or use it as a topping for pancakes, waffles, or oatmeal. Enjoy!

Red Currant and Peach Applesauce

Ingredients:

6 medium apples, peeled, cored, and sliced
2 ripe peaches, peeled, pitted, and chopped
1/2 cup fresh or frozen red currants
1/4 cup water
2 tbsps. honey
1/2 tsp. ground cinnamon

Directions:

1. In a large saucepan, combine the sliced apples, chopped peaches, red currants, and water. Bring to a boil over medium-high heat.
2. Reduce the heat to low, cover the pan, and simmer for 15-20 minutes, or until the fruit is soft and tender.
3. Remove the pan from the heat and let it cool for a few minutes.
4. Using an immersion blender or a food processor, puree the fruit until smooth.
5. Return the pan to the stove and add the honey and cinnamon. Stir to combine.
6. Cook over low heat for 5-10 minutes, stirring occasionally, until the applesauce is thickened and heated through.
7. Remove the pan from the heat and let the applesauce cool to room temperature.
8. Serve the red currant and peach applesauce as a snack or a dessert, or use it as a topping for yogurt, ice cream, or pancakes. Enjoy!

Apple Pear Applesauce

Ingredients:

6 medium apples, peeled, cored, and sliced
2 ripe pears, peeled, cored, and chopped
1/4 cup water
2 tbsps. honey
1/2 tsp. ground cinnamon
Pinch of salt

Directions:

1. In a large saucepan, combine the sliced apples, chopped pears, and water. Bring to a boil over medium-high heat.
2. Reduce the heat to low, cover the pan, and simmer for 15-20 minutes, or until the fruit is soft and tender.
3. Remove the pan from the heat and let it cool for a few minutes.
4. Using an immersion blender or a food processor, puree the fruit until smooth.
5. Return the pan to the stove and add the honey, cinnamon, and salt. Stir to combine.
6. Cook over low heat for 5-10 minutes, stirring occasionally, until the applesauce is thickened and heated through.
7. Remove the pan from the heat and let the applesauce cool to room temperature.
8. Serve the apple pear applesauce as a snack or a dessert, or use it as a topping for oatmeal, yogurt, or ice cream. Enjoy!

Strawberry Rhubarb Applesauce

Ingredients:

6 medium apples, peeled, cored, and sliced
1 cup rhubarb, chopped
1 cup strawberries, hulled and chopped
1/4 cup water
2 tbsps. honey
1/2 tsp. ground cinnamon

Directions:

1. In a large saucepan, combine the sliced apples, chopped rhubarb, chopped strawberries, and water. Bring to a boil over medium-high heat.
2. Reduce the heat to low, cover the pan, and simmer for 15-20 minutes, or until the fruit is soft and tender.
3. Remove the pan from the heat and let it cool for a few minutes.
4. Using an immersion blender or a food processor, puree the fruit until smooth.
5. Return the pan to the stove and add the honey and cinnamon. Stir to combine.
6. Cook over low heat for 5-10 minutes, stirring occasionally, until the applesauce is thickened and heated through.
7. Remove the pan from the heat and let the applesauce cool to room temperature.
8. Serve the strawberry rhubarb applesauce as a snack or a dessert, or use it as a topping for oatmeal, yogurt, or ice cream. Enjoy!

Apple Raspberry Sauce

Ingredients:

6 medium apples, peeled, cored, and sliced
1 cup fresh raspberries
1/4 cup water
2 tbsps. honey
1/2 tsp. ground cinnamon

Directions:

1. In a large saucepan, combine the sliced apples, raspberries, and water. Bring to a boil over medium-high heat.
2. Reduce the heat to low, cover the pan, and simmer for 15-20 minutes, or until the fruit is soft and tender.
3. Remove the pan from the heat and let it cool for a few minutes.
4. Using an immersion blender or a food processor, puree the fruit until smooth.
5. Return the pan to the stove and add the honey and cinnamon. Stir to combine.
6. Cook over low heat for 5-10 minutes, stirring occasionally, until the applesauce is thickened and heated through.
7. Remove the pan from the heat and let the applesauce cool to room temperature.
8. Serve the apple raspberry sauce as a snack or a dessert, or use it as a topping for oatmeal, yogurt, or ice cream. Enjoy!

Apple Cider Donuts

Donuts Ingredients:

2 cups all-purpose flour
1 tsp baking powder
1 tsp baking soda
1 tsp ground cinnamon
1/2 tsp ground nutmeg
1/4 tsp ground cloves
1/2 tsp salt
1/2 cup granulated sugar
1/2 cup apple cider
1/3 cup vegetable oil
2 large eggs
1 tsp vanilla extract

Cinnamon-Sugar Coating Ingredients:

1/2 cup granulated sugar
1 tsp ground cinnamon

Directions:

1. Preheat your oven to 350°F (175°C) and grease a donut pan.
2. In a medium bowl, whisk together the flour, baking powder, baking soda, cinnamon, nutmeg, cloves, and salt.
3. In a separate bowl, whisk together the sugar, apple cider, vegetable oil, eggs, and vanilla extract.
4. Add the dry ingredients to the wet ingredients and stir until just combined.
5. Spoon the batter into the prepared donut pan, filling each mold about 3/4 full.
6. Bake for 12-15 minutes, or until a toothpick inserted into the center of a donut comes out clean.
7. While the donuts are baking, mix together the sugar and cinnamon for the coating in a small bowl.

8. Remove the donuts from the oven and let cool in the pan for a few minutes.
9. Remove the donuts from the pan and roll them in the cinnamon-sugar mixture until coated.
10. Serve and enjoy warm or at room temperature.
11. You can store the apple cider donuts in an airtight container at room temperature for up to 3 days. Enjoy!

Apple Butter

Ingredients:

4 lbs apples (any variety), peeled and chopped
1 cup granulated sugar
1/2 cup brown sugar
1 tbsp ground cinnamon
1 tsp ground ginger
1/4 tsp ground cloves
1/4 tsp ground nutmeg
1/2 tsp salt
1/2 cup apple cider or apple juice
2 tbsp lemon juice

Directions:

1. In a large, heavy-bottomed pot, combine the chopped apples, sugars, cinnamon, ginger, cloves, nutmeg, and salt.
2. Stir in the apple cider or juice and lemon juice.
3. Cook over medium heat, stirring occasionally, until the apples are soft and tender. This should take about 30-45 minutes.
4. Using an immersion blender, puree the apple mixture until it reaches a smooth and creamy consistency.
5. Continue to cook the apple butter over low heat, stirring occasionally, for another 1-2 hours, until it has thickened and darkened in color.
6. Remove from heat and let cool for a few minutes.
7. Spoon the apple butter into sterilized jars and seal tightly.
8. Let the jars cool to room temperature, then store in the refrigerator for up to 3 months.
9. You can use apple butter as a spread on toast, as a topping for oatmeal or yogurt, or as a filling for cakes or pastries. Enjoy!

Apple Crisp

Ingredients:

6 cups thinly sliced apples (any variety)
1/2 cup all-purpose flour
1/2 cup rolled oats
1/2 cup brown sugar
1 tsp ground cinnamon
1/4 tsp ground nutmeg
1/4 tsp salt
1/2 cup unsalted butter, softened

Directions:

1. Preheat your oven to 375°F (190°C).
2. Grease an 8x8 inch baking dish with butter or cooking spray.
3. Spread the sliced apples evenly in the prepared baking dish.
4. In a medium bowl, mix together the flour, oats, brown sugar, cinnamon, nutmeg, and salt.
5. Cut in the softened butter until the mixture becomes crumbly and forms small clumps.
6. Sprinkle the crumble mixture evenly over the apples.
7. Bake for 40-45 minutes, or until the top is golden brown and the apples are tender.
8. Let cool for a few minutes before serving.

Apple Oatmeal Cookies

Ingredients:

1 cup all-purpose flour
1 cup rolled oats
1/2 tsp baking soda
1/2 tsp salt
1/2 cup unsalted butter, softened
1/2 cup granulated sugar
1/2 cup brown sugar
1 large egg
1 tsp vanilla extract
1 cup grated apple (about 1 medium apple)
1/2 cup chopped walnuts (optional)

Directions:

1. Preheat your oven to 350°F (180°C).
2. Line a baking sheet with parchment paper.
3. In a medium bowl, whisk together the flour, oats, baking soda, and salt.
4. In a separate large bowl, beat together the butter, granulated sugar, and brown sugar until light and fluffy.
5. Beat in the egg and vanilla extract until well combined.
6. Gradually stir in the dry ingredients until just combined.
7. Fold in the grated apple and chopped walnuts (if using).
8. Drop spoonfuls of dough onto the prepared baking sheet, spacing them about 2 inches apart.
9. Bake for 12-15 minutes, or until the cookies are golden brown and firm to the touch.
10. Let the cookies cool on the baking sheet for 5 minutes before transferring them to a wire rack to cool completely.

Apple Cinnamon Oatmeal Cookies

Ingredients:

2 cups all-purpose flour
1 tsp baking soda
1/2 tsp salt
1 tsp ground cinnamon
1/2 cup unsalted butter, softened
1 cup granulated sugar
1 large egg
1 tsp vanilla extract
1 cup grated apple (about 1 medium apple)
1/2 cup chopped walnuts (optional)

Directions:

1. Preheat your oven to 350°F (180°C). In a medium bowl, whisk together the flour, baking soda, salt, and cinnamon. In a separate large bowl, beat together the butter and sugar until light and fluffy. Beat in the egg and vanilla extract until well combined. Gradually stir in the dry ingredients until just combined. Fold in the grated apple and chopped walnuts (if using). Drop spoonfuls of dough onto a lined baking sheet, spacing them about 2 inches apart. Bake for 12-15 minutes, or until the cookies are golden brown and firm to the touch.

Cran-Cherry Oatmeal Cookies

Ingredients:

1 cup all-purpose flour
1 tsp ground cinnamon
1/2 tsp baking soda
1/4 tsp salt
1/2 cup unsalted butter, softened
1/2 cup granulated sugar
1/2 cup brown sugar
1 large egg
1 tsp vanilla extract
1 cup rolled oats
1/2 cup dried cranberries
1/2 cup dried cherries
1 cup grated apple (about 1 medium apple)

Directions:

1. Preheat your oven to 350°F (180°C).
2. Line a baking sheet with parchment paper.
3. In a medium bowl, whisk together the flour, cinnamon, baking soda, and salt.
4. In a separate large bowl, beat together the butter, granulated sugar, and brown sugar until light and fluffy.
5. Beat in the egg and vanilla extract until well combined.
6. Gradually stir in the dry ingredients until just combined.
7. Fold in the rolled oats, dried cranberries, dried cherries, and grated apple.
8. Drop spoonfuls of dough onto the prepared baking sheet, spacing them about 2 inches apart.
9. Bake for 12-15 minutes, or until the cookies are golden brown and firm to the touch.
10. Let the cookies cool on the baking sheet for 5 minutes before transferring them to a wire rack to cool completely.

Apple Peanut Butter Cookies

Ingredients:

1 1/2 cups all-purpose flour
1 tsp baking powder
1/2 tsp salt
1/2 cup unsalted butter, softened
1/2 cup granulated sugar
1/2 cup creamy peanut butter
1 large egg
1 tsp vanilla extract
1 cup grated apple (about 1 medium apple)

Directions:

1. Preheat your oven to 350°F (180°C). In a medium bowl, whisk together the flour, baking powder, and salt. In a separate large bowl, beat together the butter, sugar, and peanut butter until light and fluffy. Beat in the egg and vanilla extract until well combined. Gradually stir in the dry ingredients until just combined. Fold in the grated apple. Drop spoonfuls of dough onto a lined baking sheet, spacing them about 2 inches apart. Flatten each cookie with a fork in a crisscross pattern. Bake for 12-15 minutes, or until the cookies are golden brown and firm to the touch.

Apple Ginger Cookies

Ingredients:

2 cups all-purpose flour
1 tsp baking soda
1/2 tsp salt
1 tsp ground ginger
1/2 cup unsalted butter, softened
1 cup granulated sugar
1 large egg
1/4 cup molasses
1 cup grated apple (About 1 medium apple)
1/2 cup crystallized ginger, chopped

Directions:

1. Preheat your oven to 350°F (180°C). In a medium bowl, whisk together the flour, baking soda, salt, and ground ginger. In a separate large bowl, beat together the butter and sugar until light and fluffy. Beat in the egg and molasses until well combined. Gradually stir in the dry ingredients until just combined. Fold in the grated apple and crystallized ginger. Drop spoonfuls of dough onto a lined baking sheet, spacing them about 2 inches apart. Bake for 12-15 minutes, or until the cookies are golden brown and firm to the touch.

Apple Snickerdoodles

Ingredients:

2 cups all-purpose flour
1 tsp baking soda
1/2 tsp salt
1 tsp ground cinnamon
1/2 cup unsalted butter, softened
1 cup granulated sugar
1 large egg
1 tsp vanilla extract
1 cup grated apple (about 1 medium apple)
1/4 cup granulated sugar
1 tsp ground cinnamon

Directions:

1. Preheat your oven to 350°F (180°C). Line a baking sheet with parchment paper.
2. In a medium bowl, whisk together the flour, baking soda, salt, and ground cinnamon.
3. In a large bowl, beat together the butter and sugar until light and fluffy. Beat in the egg and vanilla extract until well combined.
4. Gradually stir in the dry ingredients until just combined. Fold in the grated apple.
5. In a small bowl, mix together the remaining 1/4 cup sugar and 1 tsp cinnamon.
6. Roll spoonfuls of dough into balls, then roll each ball in the cinnamon sugar mixture to coat.
7. Place the balls onto the lined baking sheet, spacing them about 2 inches apart.
8. Bake for 12-15 minutes, or until the edges are lightly browned and the centers are set.
9. Remove the cookies from the oven and let them cool on the baking sheet for

Glazed Apple Cookies

Ingredients:

2 cups all-purpose flour
1/2 tsp. baking soda
1/2 tsp. salt
1/2 tsp. ground cinnamon
1/4 tsp. ground nutmeg
1/2 cup unsalted butter, at room temperature
3/4 cup granulated sugar
1 large egg
1/2 cup unsweetened applesauce
1/2 cup chopped dried apples
1 cup powdered sugar
2 tbsps. milk
1/2 tsp. vanilla extract

Directions:

1. Preheat your oven to 350°F (180°C). Line a baking sheet with parchment paper.
2. In a medium bowl, whisk together the flour, baking soda, salt, cinnamon, and nutmeg.
3. In a large bowl, beat together the butter and granulated sugar until light and fluffy. Beat in the egg until well combined.
4. Gradually stir in the dry ingredients until just combined. Fold in the applesauce and chopped dried apples.
5. Drop spoonfuls of dough onto the lined baking sheet, spacing them about 2 inches apart.
6. Bake for 12-15 minutes, or until the cookies are golden brown and firm to the touch.
7. While the cookies are baking, whisk together the powdered sugar, milk, and vanilla extract to make the glaze.

8. Let the cookies cool on the baking sheet for 5 minutes before transferring them to a wire rack to cool completely.
9. Once the cookies are cool, drizzle the glaze over them and let it set before serving. Enjoy!

Butterscotch Apple Cookies

Ingredients:

1/2 cup unsalted butter, at room temperature
1/2 cup granulated sugar
1/2 cup light brown sugar
1 large egg
1/2 cup unsweetened applesauce
1 tsp. vanilla extract
2 cups all-purpose flour
1 tsp. baking soda
1/2 tsp. salt
1 cup butterscotch chips
1 cup chopped dried apples

Directions:

1. Preheat your oven to 375°F (190°C). Line a baking sheet with parchment paper.
2. In a large bowl, beat together the butter, granulated sugar, and light brown sugar until light and fluffy.
3. Beat in the egg until well combined, then stir in the applesauce and vanilla extract.
4. In a separate bowl, whisk together the flour, baking soda, and salt.
5. Gradually stir the dry ingredients into the wet mixture until just combined.
6. Fold in the butterscotch chips and chopped dried apples.
7. Drop spoonfuls of dough onto the lined baking sheet, spacing them about 2 inches apart.
8. Bake for 10-12 minutes, or until the cookies are lightly golden brown and firm to the touch.
9. Let the cookies cool on the baking sheet for 5 minutes before transferring them to a wire rack to cool completely. Enjoy!

Apple Squares

Ingredients:

2 cups all-purpose flour
1/2 cup granulated sugar
1/2 cup unsalted butter, at room temperature
1 large egg
1/4 tsp. salt
4 cups peeled and chopped apples (about 4 medium apples)
1/2 cup light brown sugar
2 tsps. ground cinnamon
1/4 tsp. ground nutmeg
1/4 cup unsalted butter, melted

Directions:

1. Preheat your oven to 350°F (180°C). Grease a 9-inch square baking pan.
2. In a large bowl, beat together the flour, granulated sugar, and butter until crumbly.
3. Beat in the egg and salt until well combined.
4. Press about two-thirds of the dough mixture evenly into the bottom of the prepared pan.
5. In a medium bowl, mix together the chopped apples, brown sugar, cinnamon, and nutmeg.
6. Spread the apple mixture evenly over the dough in the pan.
7. Crumble the remaining dough mixture over the top of the apple mixture.
8. Drizzle the melted butter over the crumbled dough.
9. Bake for 35-40 minutes, or until the top is golden brown and the apples are tender.
10. Let the apple squares cool in the pan for 10 minutes before cutting them into squares and serving. Enjoy!

Golden Apple Raisin Squares

Ingredients:

2 cups all-purpose flour
1/2 cup granulated sugar
1/2 cup unsalted butter, at room temperature
1 large egg
1/4 tsp. salt
2 cups peeled and chopped apples (about 2 medium apples)
1/2 cup raisins
1/4 cup honey
1/4 cup unsalted butter, melted
1 tsp. ground cinnamon

Directions:

1. Preheat your oven to 350°F (180°C). Grease a 9-inch square baking pan.
2. In a large bowl, beat together the flour, granulated sugar, and butter until crumbly.
3. Beat in the egg and salt until well combined.
4. Press about two-thirds of the dough mixture evenly into the bottom of the prepared pan.
5. In a medium bowl, mix together the chopped apples, raisins, honey, melted butter, and cinnamon.
6. Spread the apple mixture evenly over the dough in the pan.
7. Crumble the remaining dough mixture over the top of the apple mixture.
8. Bake for 35-40 minutes, or until the top is golden brown and the apples are tender.
9. Let the apple squares cool in the pan for 10 minutes before cutting them into squares and serving. Enjoy!

Upside-Down Double Apple Coffee Cake

Topping Ingredients:

1/4 cup unsalted butter
1/2 cup packed light brown sugar
1/4 tsp. ground cinnamon
2 large apples, peeled and thinly sliced

Cake Ingredients:

2 cups all-purpose flour
1 tbsp. baking powder
1/2 tsp. baking soda
1/4 tsp. salt
1/2 cup unsalted butter, at room temperature
1 cup granulated sugar
2 large eggs
1 tsp. vanilla extract
1 cup unsweetened applesauce
1/2 cup sour cream

Directions:

1. Preheat your oven to 350°F (180°C). Grease a 9-inch round cake pan.
2. For the topping, melt the butter in a small saucepan over medium heat. Add the brown sugar and cinnamon and stir until the sugar has dissolved. Pour the mixture into the prepared cake pan, spreading it evenly to cover the bottom. Arrange the apple slices on top of the brown sugar mixture.
3. For the cake, in a medium bowl, whisk together the flour, baking powder, baking soda, and salt.
4. In a large bowl, beat together the butter and granulated sugar until light and fluffy. Add the eggs, one at a time, beating well after each addition. Stir in the vanilla extract.

5. In a small bowl, whisk together the applesauce and sour cream. Add this mixture to the butter-sugar mixture, and stir until well combined.
6. Gradually stir in the flour mixture until just combined. Do not overmix.
7. Pour the batter evenly over the apples in the prepared pan.
8. Bake for 45-50 minutes, or until a toothpick inserted in the center comes out clean.
9. Let the coffee cake cool in the pan for 10 minutes. Then, run a knife around the edge of the pan to loosen the cake. Place a serving plate upside down over the pan and invert the cake onto the plate.
10. Serve warm or at room temperature. Enjoy!

Pumpkin Apple Cobbler

Filling Ingredients:

4 cups apples, peeled, cored, and sliced
1 cup pumpkin puree
1/2 cup brown sugar
1/4 cup granulated sugar
2 tbsps. cornstarch
1 tsp. ground cinnamon
1/2 tsp. ground nutmeg
1/4 tsp. ground ginger
1/4 tsp. salt

Topping Ingredients:

1 cup all-purpose flour
1/4 cup granulated sugar
1/4 cup brown sugar
1 tsp. baking powder
1/2 tsp. ground cinnamon
1/4 tsp. salt
1/2 cup unsalted butter, cold and cubed
1/4 cup milk

Directions:

1. Preheat the oven to 375°F (190°C). Grease a 9-inch baking dish with nonstick cooking spray.
2. In a large bowl, combine the sliced apples, pumpkin puree, brown sugar, granulated sugar, cornstarch, cinnamon, nutmeg, ginger, and salt. Mix well.
3. Pour the apple pumpkin mixture into the prepared baking dish.
4. In another bowl, combine the flour, granulated sugar, brown sugar, baking powder, cinnamon, and salt. Mix well.

5. Add the cubed butter to the flour mixture and use your fingers or a pastry cutter to mix until the mixture resembles coarse crumbs.
6. Stir in the milk until the mixture forms a thick batter.
7. Drop spoonfuls of the batter over the apple pumpkin mixture, covering the surface as evenly as possible.
8. Bake the cobbler for 45-50 minutes, or until the topping is golden brown and the filling is bubbly.
9. Remove the cobbler from the oven and let it cool for 10-15 minutes before serving.
10. Serve the pumpkin apple cobbler warm with a scoop of vanilla ice cream or whipped cream on top. Enjoy!

Butterscotch Apple Pecan Cobbler

Filling Ingredients:

6 cups apples, peeled, cored, and sliced
1/2 cup butterscotch chips
1/2 cup chopped pecans
1/4 cup all-purpose flour
1/4 cup brown sugar
1/4 cup granulated sugar
1 tsp. ground cinnamon
1/4 tsp. salt

Topping Ingredients:

1 cup all-purpose flour
1/4 cup brown sugar
1/4 cup granulated sugar
1 tsp. baking powder
1/2 tsp. ground cinnamon
1/4 tsp. salt
1/2 cup unsalted butter, cold and cubed
1/4 cup milk

Directions:

1. Preheat the oven to 375°F (190°C). Grease a 9-inch baking dish with nonstick cooking spray.
2. In a large bowl, combine the sliced apples, butterscotch chips, chopped pecans, flour, brown sugar, granulated sugar, cinnamon, and salt. Mix well.
3. Pour the apple mixture into the prepared baking dish.
4. In another bowl, combine the flour, brown sugar, granulated sugar, baking powder, cinnamon, and salt. Mix well.
5. Add the cubed butter to the flour mixture and use your fingers or a pastry cutter to mix until the mixture resembles coarse crumbs.
6. Stir in the milk until the mixture forms a thick batter.

7. Drop spoonfuls of the batter over the apple mixture, covering the surface as evenly as possible.
8. Bake the cobbler for 45-50 minutes, or until the topping is golden brown and the filling is bubbly.
9. Remove the cobbler from the oven and let it cool for 10-15 minutes before serving.
10. Serve the butterscotch apple pecan cobbler warm with a scoop of vanilla ice cream or whipped cream on top. Enjoy!

About the Author

Laura Sommers is **The Recipe Lady!**

She lives on a small farm in Baltimore County, Maryland and has a passion for food. She has taken cooking classes in New York City, Memphis, New Orleans and Washington DC. She has been a taste tester for a large spice company in Baltimore and written food reviews for several local papers. She loves writing cookbooks with the most delicious recipes to share her knowledge and love of cooking with the world.

Follow her on Pinterest:

http://pinterest.com/therecipelady1

Visit the Recipe Lady's blog for even more great recipes:

http://the-recipe-lady.blogspot.com/

Visit her Amazon Author Page to see her latest books:

amazon.com/author/laurasommers

Follow the Recipe Lady on Facebook:

https://www.facebook.com/therecipegirl

Follow her on Twitter:

https://twitter.com/TheRecipeLady1

Other Books by Laura Sommers

Irish Recipes for St. Patrick's Day

Traditional Vermont Recipes

Traditional Memphis Recipes

Maryland Chesapeake Bay Blue Crab Cookbook

Mussels Cookbook

Maryland Chesapeake Bay Blue Crab Cookbook

Salmon Cookbook

Scallop Recipes